Who Invented the
Computer?

Who Invented the Computer?

Robert Snedden

ARCTURUS

This edition first published in 2010 by Arcturus Publishing
Distributed by Black Rabbit Books
P.O. Box 3263
Mankato
Minnesota MN 56002

Printed in China

Planned and produced by Discovery Books Ltd.
www.discoverybooks.net
Managing editor: Laura Durman
Editors: Clare Collinson and Jenny Vaughan
Designer: Ian Winton
Illustrator: Stefan Chabluk

Library of Congress Cataloging-in-Publication Data

Snedden, Robert.
  Who invented the computer? / Robert Snedden.
      p. cm. – (Breakthroughs in science and technology)
  Includes index.
  Summary: "Looking at some of the major inventions and discoveries shaping our world today, Breakthroughs in Science profiles the research leading up to the discovery (not just profiles of the one or two key "players"). Each book describes the "famous" moment and then examines the continued evolution illustrating its impact today and for the future"–Provided by publisher.
  ISBN 978-1-84837-678-6 (library binding)
  1. Computers–Juvenile literature. I. Title.
  QA76.23.S58 2011
  004–dc22
                                   2010011017

Picture Credits
BBN Technologies: 36. The Bletchley Park Trust www.bletchleypark.org.uk: 20. Corbis: 14 (Stefano Bianchetti), 19 (Bettmann), 21, 23 (Jerry Cooke). Getty Images: 6 (Don Smetzer), 7 (Hulton Archive), 8 (SSPL), 10 (The Bridgeman Art Library), 11 (Janek Skarzynski/AFP), 12 (SSPL), 15 top (SSPL), 25 (Time & Life Pictures), 29 (SSPL), 30 (Hulton Archive), 31 (Bettmann), 35 top (Apic/Hulton Archive). IBM: 38. Library of Congress: 15 bottom (C M Bell). MOSI: 26 (Chris Foster). Nokia: 16. Rex Features: 24 (20th Century Fox/Everett). Science Photo Library: 28 (Emilio Segre Visual Archives/American Institute of Physics). Shutterstock Images: title page and 43 (Monkey Business Images), 18 (Jozsef Szasz-Fabian), 35 bottom (Alexander Kalina), 37 (Christopher Futcher), 41 (3777190317), 42 (Eray Haciosmanoglu). Courtesy Texas Instruments: 32, 33. Wikimedia Commons: 9, 13, 27 (Daderot), 39, 40 (Michael Holley). Courtesy of Horst Zuse: 18.

SL001444US   Supplier 03, Date 0510

Contents

It all adds up!

Computer life

Computers are one of the most common gadgets we use in everyday life. Most households in the developed world now own one, and they are found in most schools and libraries. We use them to store our music and photographs, research homework, shop, play games, and keep in touch with friends. This versatile tool came about through our need to count things.

Count on it

People have been counting for many thousands of years. However, doing so exactly and making calculations has always presented problems, as people often lose track of what they are doing, and make mistakes. For this reason, they have looked for ways to help them get calculations right.

The earliest known counting device is the beaded frame called the **abacus**, which was invented about 3,000 years ago. It is still used today in many parts of the world. An abacus is not a calculator. The operator

The abacus is still used in many countries today. Here, a Korean storekeeper uses an abacus to find out the total price of the goods he is selling. Each stage of a calculation is recorded by moving beads across the frame.

John Napier

Date of birth: 1550 (exact date not known)

Place of birth: Edinburgh, Scotland

Profession: Mathematician

Greatest achievement: The discovery of logarithms

Interesting fact: There is a story that Napier wanted to catch a servant who had been stealing. He put a rooster in a dark shed, and said that the bird would identify the guilty person. Each man had to go and stroke the bird. Napier, guessing that the thief would be afraid to touch it, had covered the bird with soot. The thief would be the only one to emerge with clean hands!

Date of death: April 4, 1617

still has to do the math in his or her head, but moving the beads to different positions on the frame helps keep track of each stage of a calculation.

Logarithms

For thousands of years, using an abacus was the best way to do calculations. Then in 1614 John Napier, a Scottish mathematician, discovered **logarithms**.

Logarithms make it possible to turn multiplication into addition. To multiply two numbers, you look up the logarithm for each in list of numbers called a table and add them together. (Adding is easier than multiplying.)

Logarithms had a huge impact on science. The astronomer Johannes Kepler, for example, had written about how he was driven to distraction by the calculations he had to do. Logarithms made his work, and that of other scientists, much simpler. They remained in use for more than three centuries until mechanical calculators and, eventually, computers replaced them.

Calculators

Living computers

During the 16th to 18th centuries, more and more of the world was being explored by Europeans. The resulting trade boom was known as the "Commercial Revolution." The increase in travel and trade meant that faster ways of making calculations were needed.

The word "computer" was first used around the same time as Napier was discovering logarithms. These computers weren't machines: they were people who made calculations (or **computations**). These could include calculating the positions of stars and planets, for use in ships' navigation charts.

Humans doing calculations all day may get bored, tired, and make mistakes. So inventors looked for ways of making the task of computing faster and more reliable. The search for a practical mechanical computer was on.

The calculating clock

In 1617, the year Napier died, German churchman Wilhelm Schickard met the astronomer Johannes Kepler and the two men became friends. Kepler was using Napier's logarithms as he studied the stars and planets, but Schickard

Although the original "calculating clock" was destroyed, Schickard left a detailed enough description of it for this replica to be built. It is in the Deutsches Museum in Munich, Germany.

wanted to make a machine for him that would automate the process. In 1623, he built a device that he called a "calculating clock." This was the first mechanical calculator. Unfortunately, before he could give it to Kepler, it was destroyed in a fire.

The Pascaline

The first mechanical calculator to be produced and actually used was the arithmetic machine, or Pascaline, designed by French mathematician Blaise Pascal in 1645. Numbers were entered into the machine by turning a series of dials. Pascal designed the machine to help his father, a tax collector. Pascal built 50 arithmetic machines, and managed to sell about a dozen of them. In 1671, German mathematician Gottfried Wilhelm von Leibniz designed a machine called the step reckoner. This was an improvement on Pascal's idea, because, by adding numbers repeatedly, it could multiply.

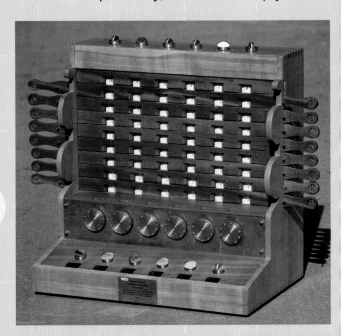

Blaise Pascal

Date of birth: June 19, 1623

Place of birth: Clermont, France

Profession: Mathematician and philosopher

Greatest achievement: Pascal is best known for developing a mathematical theory, called the theory of **probability**.

Interesting fact: Pascal set out an argument for believing in God, called "Pascal's wager." He said that if God does not exist, one will lose nothing by believing in him. But if God does exist, one will lose everything by not believing.

Date of death: August 19, 1662

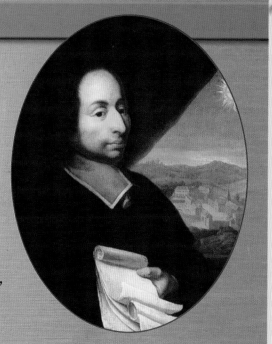

The binary system

As well as making his step reckoner, Leibniz was also interested in the **binary number system** and how it could be used.

In everyday life, we use the decimal system of counting. The decimal, or "base 10," system uses the numbers 1 to 9 and 0. Numbers are ordered in multiples of ten: units in one column, tens in the next, hundreds in the next, and so on. The binary system uses just two symbols, 0 and 1. So "1" is written as 1, but "2" is written as 10—meaning one 2 and no 1s. Three is 11—one 2 and one 1. Four is two 2s, which is 100 (just as 10 tens are 100 in the decimal system). Five is 101 (two 2s and one 1)—and so on.

Today, binary is the cornerstone of **computer programming**, where every number can be represented by a series of switches that are either on (1), or off (0).

0 =	0
1 =	1
2 =	10
3 =	11
4 =	100
5 =	101
6 =	110
7 =	111
8 =	1000
9 =	1001
10 =	1010

This table shows the numbers 1 to 10 in the decimal system we use every day, and how they are written in the binary system.

Breakthrough

Mechanical calculators were invented, making calculations easier and more likely to be accurate. This was important both in science and trade.

A revolution

Industry arrives

The Commercial Revolution was followed in the late 18th and early 19th centuries by the **Industrial Revolution**—one of the most important periods in human history. It began in Britain around 1730, and it was a time when there was a shift from a largely rural economy where everything was made by hand, to one with large cities and factories producing goods in huge quantities.

The Jacquard loom

Textile manufacture was one of the principal industries of the Industrial Revolution, and this was one of the first things to be mechanized. In 1804,

The Industrial Revolution brought a massive increase in manufacturing and trade. There was an urgent need for fast, easy to use, accurate calculating machines to keep track of the goods being produced, and the money changing hands.

Frenchman Joseph-Marie Jacquard invented a textile-weaving loom. It was one of the most ingenious devices of its time and introduced a technology that was still in use 150 years later, including in early computers: **punched cards**.

Punched cards

Like other looms, the Jacquard had a series of threads running lengthways (the warp threads), and a shuttle that carried another thread back and forth (the weft thread), weaving in and out of these to make the cloth. Patterns were created by raising and lowering individual warp threads, so that the weft was sometimes in front of the warp thread and sometimes behind it.

Jacquard's loom used hooks to raise and lower the warp threads. These were controlled by a series of cards with rows of holes punched in them. Where a hook met

a hole in a card, it could pass through and raise the thread. Where there was no hole, the hook was stopped and the thread stayed down. One row of holes on the card corresponded to a single pass of the shuttle across the warp threads. A whole deck of these punched cards could be inserted into a device that automatically dropped cards into place, one at a time, making it possible to weave very complicated patterns. In effect, the cards "programmed" the loom to weave patterns automatically. It was the first machine ever to be operated in this way.

A Jacquard loom in use in Poland. Punched cards carry the instructions that control the way the cloth is woven. Patterns are automatically produced, using the different colored threads.

The arithmometer

With the changes in manufacturing brought about by mechanization, and the boom in national and international trade that followed, the need for better, faster, and more reliable calculating devices grew ever stronger. This was because merchants had to keep track of so many goods and materials and so much money was changing hands.

Frenchman Charles Xavier Thomas de Colmar invented the first commercial calculator in 1820. The arithmometer, as it was called, used a system of sliders to input the numbers and dials to show the answers. It could reliably add, subtract, and multiply and, with a bit of effort from the user, it could divide, too. Production began in 1851 and continued, with improvements, until 1914, when the company went out of business.

Breakthroughs

Inventors had found ways to program machines to carry out complicated tasks without humans being present. Calculating machines became widely available commercially and made the task of buying and selling on a vast scale much easier.

Babbage and his engines

The problem with tables

In the days before calculators became commonplace, scientists, navigators, tax collectors, engineers, and others all relied on mathematical tables (such as logarithms) to help solve problems. The tables set out the results of various mathematical calculations. Human computers compiled these tables, and they often made mistakes. So did the printers who printed them.

The Difference Engine

The English mathematician Charles Babbage was fascinated by mathematical tables and owned a 300-volume collection of them. In 1821, he set out to find a reliable way of mechanizing the process of producing accurate tables.

Between 1991 and 2000, staff at the Science Museum in London, UK, used Charles Babbage's designs to build a working Difference Engine. They were able to do this because modern technology could produce the parts accurately—something that was impossible in Babbage's time.

Babbage's first design was for what he called a Difference Engine. Unlike the calculators of Schickard and others, this wasn't intended to be used for arithmetic problems but to generate mathematical tables. A full-size Difference Engine would have needed 25,000 parts, and every one of them had to be made by hand, using customized tools. It proved to be too great a challenge for the engineers of the time and, in 1833, the Difference Engine was abandoned, still incomplete.

The Analytical Engine

Babbage next planned a machine that could be programmed to perform any

Ada, Countess of Lovelace

Ada, the Countess of Lovelace, was the daughter of the poet, Lord Byron. Ada is often called the "first **programmer**," because she wrote a series of instructions that would have been used to operate the Analytical Engine. Babbage referred to her as the "Enchantress of Numbers." In her notes she was farsighted enough to predict the possibility of computer-generated music.

"The Analytical Engine weaves algebraic patterns, just as the Jacquard loom weaves flowers and leaves."
Ada, Countess of Lovelace, 1843.

calculation. He called this an Analytical Engine. It made even more demands of engineers than the Difference Engine. Only test models of small sections of it were ever built.

The designs for the Analytical Engine included features that would become common in modern computers. It could be programmed using punched cards similar to those that operated Jacquard's loom. It had a store, where numbers and partial results could be held, similar to the **memory** in a computer today. A separate part of the engine, called the mill, was the place where the actual calculations were performed. It was like the central processor of a modern computer. Had Babbage actually built an Analytical Engine, it would have been the world's first computer as we understand it.

Breakthrough

Charles Babbage's great breakthrough was the idea that a machine could be programmed to carry out calculations.

Information processing

Counting people

As the 19th century progressed, businesses and governments needed to handle more and more information. Many countries held a census (a count of the population) every 10 years (as they do now). This was particularly important in the United States, where mass immigration was increasing population dramatically. By 1880, the U.S. census was gathering so much data that it took nearly 10 years to publish the results. Someone had to find a way to mechanize the process.

Hermann Hollerith

That person turned out to be Herman Hollerith. Hollerith, who had worked on the epic 1880 census, began to look for better ways of handling the census data.

He carried out his first experiments while he was teaching at the Massachusetts Institute of Technology in 1882. He devised a way to automate data collection, using punched cards. Although the cards looked very similar to those used by the Jacquard loom, Hollerith's inspiration actually came from watching train and bus conductors punch holes in tickets. The holes in the cards matched the answers to questions on the census, and the technology also made use of the sensation of the day—electricity.

Hollerith developed methods to convert the information on the cards into electrical impulses. A machine called a tabulator was equipped with a number of spring-loaded pins. Punched cards were fed into the readers and, whenever a pin passed through a hole in a card, it completed an electrical circuit. This activated a mechanical counter.

This illustration shows immigrants arriving in New York. Around 25 million immigrants arrived in the United States between 1860 and 1920. It was vital for the government to keep track of this population.

A 1960s' model of Herman Hollerith's tabulator. A machine like this, which sorted information recorded on punched cards, was used to gather data from the 1890 census.

Using the tabulator, the census gatherers were able to find numbers of particular groups of people—for example, how many 30-to-40-year-old, white, male bus drivers lived in Chicago.

The Electric Tabulating System

Hollerith called his system the Electric Tabulating System. It handled information so quickly that it won the competition for the contract to handle the 1890 census data. The first data arrived in September 1890. Counting was complete by December. This was an astonishing advancement in speed and efficiency.

Birth of a giant

There was soon a great demand for Hollerith's machines. In 1896, he set up the Tabulating Machine Company. In 1911, he joined forces with other companies and together they eventually became the International Business Machines Corporation (IBM). It grew to become one of the giants of the computer world, and it still is today.

Herman Hollerith

Date of birth: February 29, 1860

Place of birth: Buffalo, New York

Profession: Inventor

Greatest achievement: Hollerith's inventions were the foundation of the modern information processing industry.

Interesting fact: Hollerith's great passion was not technology, but farming. In 1921, he escaped the "mean business" and kept a farm with his wife and children.

Date of death: November 17, 1929

Pressing keys

As the 20th century approached, business machines continued to develop. The first commercial typewriter appeared in 1874 and, in 1887, Dorr E. Felt patented the first calculator to be operated by pressing keys rather than turning a handle or setting dials. This meant that a skilled operator could do very rapid calculations.

The vacuum tube

In 1904, John Ambrose Fleming of University College London, UK, made the first practical **vacuum tube**. This invention would have an important effect on computer development.

Vacuum tubes provided a more efficient way of controlling the flow of electricity than anything previously invented. They were made of glass, sealed tight with a vacuum inside. Each tube contained fine threads, called filaments, as in old-fashioned **incandescent lightbulbs**. When the filaments are heated they release electrons (tiny particles of atoms), which are drawn to a small metal plate, also inside the tube. This is a flow of electricity, and leads extend out of the tube to carry this current.

In 1906, American inventor Lee De Forest invented a type of vacuum tube called a

The 20th century saw a massive increase in the use of office machines. The layout of keys developed for use on early typewriters is still used in modern computing, and even in some cell phones.

triode. The triode also had a small grid contained in the tube that amplified the voltage and allowed the flow between the filament and plate to be varied. For the next 40 years the vacuum tube would be an essential part of all electronic equipment.

THAT'S A FACT!

Just as valves in pipes allow water to flow only one way or another, so the vacuum tube only allows electricity to do the same. For this reason, vacuum tubes are often also called valves.

Flip-flop

In 1918, British physicists Frank W. Jordan and William H. Eccles found a way to wire two triodes together to form a type of electronic switch. This is a "flip-flop" circuit. Depending on how a current is applied, the circuit will flip from one output to another. This would form the basis of computer memory because computers store information and instructions using the binary system (see page 9). This means that anything with two distinct forms (like the flip-flop circuit) can represent the binary ones and zeros: one output will stand for one, the other for zero.

The stage was set for the invention of the electronic computer. In the 1930s, the technology would finally come together in what was to be called the "First Age of Computing."

Vacuum tubes were developed at the beginning of the 20th century and were used in all electronic equipment, including radios, televisions, and early computers. They were eventually replaced by transistors from the mid-1940s onward.

Breakthrough

The vacuum tube, or valve, was a vital part of all electronic equipment until the invention of the transistor (see page 28).

Relays and switches

Binary breakthrough

Even while World War II (1939–45) was threatening to engulf the world, scientists continued to develop more and more sophisticated calculating machines. Over a period of just a few years, researchers and engineers brought together the technology of the vacuum tube with the binary system of counting to produce the world's first electronic computers.

Zuse's bedroom

Konrad Zuse was a German aircraft engineer. As a student, he had dreamed of having a machine to help him with the lengthy and boring calculations he had to perform. In 1936, he resigned from his job to build that machine. He started working on it in his bedroom, but his invention soon grew so large that it spilled out into his parents' living room as well. The Z1, as it was called, was entirely mechanical, and not very reliable, but was the first calculating device to be based on the binary system.

As World War II began, Zuse continued his work, making the Z2, an improvement on the Z1. In 1941, financed by friends and partly backed by the German government, he made the world's first electronic, fully programmable digital computer, the Z3. It operated using 2,000 electrically operated switches, called **relays**, which came mostly from discarded telephone stock. The first Z3 was destroyed in a bombing raid of Berlin in 1945, though Zuse rebuilt it later.

As easy as ABC

While Zuse was working on his computers, John Atanasoff and Clifford Berry, both at Iowa State University, were developing ideas of their own. Instead of electrically operated relay switches, however, they were experimenting with vacuum tubes.

Konrad Zuse works on a replica model of his invention, the Z1, which he decided to rebuild in 1986.

Howard Aiken with his Harvard Mark I, which he said was a modern version of Babbage's Analytical Engine. It could work for hours without human intervention, making a noise, according to Lieutenant Grace Hopper, like "a thousand knitting needles."

In late 1939, they built the first binary computer that used electricity and vacuum tubes—the Atanasoff Berry Computer, or ABC. The final model of the ABC could make one calculation every 15 seconds, roughly 150 billion times slower than a modern computer.

> *"I have always taken the position that there is enough credit for everyone in the invention and development of the electronic computer."*
> John Atanasoff, 1973

THAT'S A FACT!

Grace Hopper, who worked with Aiken on the Mark I, is responsible for a computer fault being called a "bug." The original bug was actually a moth that got stuck inside the Mark I. Hopper, removed the moth, and so became the first person to "debug" a computer.

The Harvard Mark I

Around the same time, Howard Aiken, an inventor working at Harvard University in Cambridge, Massachusetts, was developing digital calculators. He had read about Babbage's Analytical Engine and made plans to build a calculating machine that would make use of the advances in technology that had taken place since Babbage's time.

Aiken's first fully functional computer, the Harvard Mark I, was built between 1939 and 1944. It was a 5 ton (4.5 t) giant, with three-quarters of a million parts and hundreds of miles of wiring. It was programmed using a card-punch, two punched-card readers, three paper tape readers, and two typewriters. It was the earliest form of the digital computer—that is, the first calculator controlled by programming. The US Navy used it until 1959, for calculating gunnery ranges.

Breakthrough

The Z3, the ABC, and the Mark I were the first electronic digital computers. They paved the way for the electronic revolution that was to come.

Codebreakers

While Aiken and his colleagues were building computers in the United States, World War II was well under way in Europe. Secrecy plays a vital part in war, as each side tries to ensure that its plans are kept out of the other's hands. This is often done by sending communications in **code**.

In the years before, and during, World War II, the German military coded their messages using a device called Enigma to send messages. Computers would have a part to play in breaking these codes.

The Enigma machine used a series of rotating wheels to change text into code. As the message was typed into the machine, the wheels rotated with every press of the keys. This meant that the letters in the message were coded differently each time, making the code very hard to break. To read the message, you had to know how the wheels were set up to generate the code. In fact, the Enigma code was broken by Polish codebreakers in the early 1930s. In 1939, fearing a German invasion, they turned their knowledge over to the British.

The Enigma was one of the most famous coding devices used in World War II. A message typed into it emerged in a code so complex that the Germans believed—wrongly— that it would be impossible to decipher.

Ultra

In early 1939, Britain's Secret Service set up the Ultra codebreaking project at Bletchley Park, to the north of London, UK. Its job was to intercept and decode Enigma messages. Ultra was classified top secret and great care was taken to make sure that the Germans wouldn't learn that the Allies knew what their plans were.

At Bletchley Park, two mathematicians, Alan Turing and Gordon Welchman, developed a codebreaking machine they

D-day—the Allied invasion of Normandy—took place in June 1944. The work of the codebreaking team at Bletchley Park, and the Colossus decoding machine, played an important part in this chapter of World War II.

called the Bombe to read messages sent in the Enigma code. It worked like this:

- It was known that no letter could be coded as itself on the Enigma machine.
- It was also known that coded messages often contained common words. This allowed codebreakers to make guesses, or "cribs," to find out what these words were and what letters they contained.
- The Bombe was wired up according to the cribs and set running. It worked through all the possible letter combinations for the remaining words.

Lorenz and Colossus

The Enigma machine used three wheels to generate code. The Lorenz machine, which the German military commanders used for high-level communications, had 12. The British codebreakers found out how to break the code, but it took so long to decipher a message that the information it contained was useless. The Bletchley Park team faced the challenge of building a machine to mechanize the process. Tommy (later Sir Thomas)

Flowers, an engineer working for the Royal Post Office in the UK, directed this work.

The resulting machine, Colossus, was completed in 1943. It read paper tape at a rate of 5,000 characters a second. Colossus was one of the forerunners of the computers of today. The messages it deciphered were vitally important in planning the D-day invasion of Europe.

THAT'S A FACT!

Colossus was enormous: it was 16.4 feet (5 m) long, 9.8 feet (3 m) deep, and 8.2 feet (2.5 m) high, and was constructed from telephone exchange parts.

Breakthrough

Colossus proved that computers could be made powerful enough to tackle complex calculations, and to work through problems much faster than people could.

ENIAC

Accurate artillery

The United States entered World War II in late 1941. One thing the US military wanted to be sure of was that its artillery was as accurate as possible. The army turned to the country's scientists and engineers for help. It commissioned a computer that would precisely calculate firing ranges for artillery under different types of conditions.

A computer for war

Work on the new computer began on May 31, 1943 at the Moore School of Electrical Engineering in Pennsylvania. The chief consultant was John W. Mauchly and the chief engineer was John Presper Eckert.

After the war

It took the team two-and-a-half years to design and build the Electronic Numerical Integrator and Calculator (ENIAC). By that time, it had cost half a million dollars— and the war was over. However, other uses were found for ENIAC, including weather prediction, designing wind tunnels for aircraft tests, and doing calculations for the design of a hydrogen bomb.

Until now, computers followed their instructions one after another, from beginning to end. ENIAC was able to change the order in which it did things. It used vacuum tubes instead of switches,

THAT'S A FACT!

ENIAC contained 17,468 vacuum tubes, 70,000 resistors, 1,500 relays, 6,000 manual switches, and 5 million soldered joints. It took up about 1,800 square feet (167 sq m) of floor space, weighed 30 tons (27 t), and consumed 160 kilowatts of electrical power. In one second, ENIAC could carry out 5,000 additions or 357 multiplications.

which meant it could operate very quickly. It could also be reprogrammed to carry out different tasks—but this was such a time-consuming process that it could take weeks.

This was because ENIAC used plugboards (as did Colossus) rather than punched-card readers for programming. Plugboards were the forerunners of **software** programming. They contained wires that could function as switches by closing a circuit, or could direct data from one part of the computer to another. The wiring could be very complicated, and the end result looked rather as if someone had thrown two plates of spaghetti at the computer. With just one plug out of place, the whole program could fail.

An employee tests the ENIAC computer in 1947. Its complicated wiring can clearly be seen. Although ENIAC may look cumbersome to us, in its time, it represented the cutting edge of electronic technology.

The unreliable vacuum

The vacuum tubes ENIAC used produced a great deal of heat. A powerful air-conditioning system had to be used to keep ENIAC cool. Also, the tubes were prone to fail. Several burned out every day when ENIAC first operated. Many improvements in vacuum tube design were made as a result of the work done on ENIAC.

Breakthrough

ENIAC showed that it was possible to build big, reliable computers. This encouraged other scientists and engineers to get involved in computing.

Crucial developments

Mathematicians

In the immediate postwar period, two mathematicians played crucial roles in the development of computers. One was Alan Turing, who helped design the equipment used at Bletchley Park (see page 20). The other was Hungarian-born American, John von Neumann.

Artificial intelligence

Turing is often described as the "father of **artificial intelligence**," the science that explores the possibility of creating "thinking" machines. In 1950, he came up with a test to determine whether a machine was intelligent:

• Questions are put to a person and a machine in another room—without the

> "I believe that in about 50 years' time . . . one will be able to speak of machines thinking without expecting to be contradicted."
> Alan Turing, 1950.

questioner knowing which is answering. The questioning and answering is carried out via computer keyboards and screens so there are no "voice" clues.

• If the questioner cannot tell from the answers whether a computer or a human

Turing's idea of a machine being "intelligent" was taken to the extreme in the 2004 movie _I, Robot_ starring Will Smith. In the movie, set in 2035, a unique robot called Sonny (left) is not only able to think for himself, but also to feel emotions.

Alan Turing

Date of birth: June 23, 1912

Place of birth: London, England

Profession: Mathematician

Greatest achievement: Pioneer thinker on artificial intelligence and computers

Interesting fact: Turing was homosexual at a time when it was a crime in Britain. When this was discovered in 1952 he was judged a security risk and lost access to work on codes and computers. He died of cyanide poisoning (possibly suicide) in 1954.

Date of death: June 7, 1954

is responding, then the computer can be said to be intelligent.

Computer scientists still try to design computers and programs that can pass Turing's test.

The stored-program computer

In 1946, John von Neumann published a paper that is sometimes referred to as the "birth certificate of computer science." He came up with the idea that a computer's data and its instructions should be kept in a single store. This was the stored-program computer. Storing instructions within a computer meant they could be accessed quickly, without needing to be fed in via paper cards or plugboards.

Von Neumann also wanted to code the instructions so that they could be modified by other instructions. This was a big step forward, and most advances in writing computer software came about as a result of von Neumann's idea.

The way computer components are connected is called the computer architecture. Von Neumann invented the arrangement of computer components used in almost every computer today. The first computer to be built according to the principles suggested by von Neumann was the Manchester Baby (see next page).

Breakthrough

Turing's work on artificial intelligence, and von Neumann's on computer architecture, influenced the way computers developed for years to come.

A first

The Small Scale Experimental Machine, nicknamed the "Baby," successfully executed its first program in 1948 at the University of Manchester, UK. Baby took von Neumann's idea of a computer that could store its own programs and made it a reality. Alan Turing wrote one of the first programs for the Baby.

The Williams-Kilburn tube

Baby was built to test a new storage device called the Williams-Kilburn tube. This was a type of **cathode ray tube**, invented by the British engineer, Sir Frederic Williams. In the tube, information was stored as tiny areas of **electric charge** on a phosphor-coated screen. These made bright and dark dots on the screen, which represented binary numbers (bright = 1, dark = 0). The tube was the first "random access" storage system. This meant that the computer could access any of its stored data quickly, without having to read through everything in sequence.

Sir Frederic Williams

Date of birth: June 26, 1911

Place of birth: Stockport, England

Profession: Engineer

Greatest achievement: The invention of the Williams-Kilburn tube

Interesting fact: Williams pioneered the first fully automatic radar system for fighter aircraft.

Date of death: August 11, 1977

As a stored-program computer, Baby could be reprogrammed in hours rather than the days it took for ENIAC. After a few false starts, Baby ran successfully and, as its inventor Frederic Williams said, "nothing was ever the same again."

RAM and ROM

A computer's memory can be divided into main (or primary) memory, known as **random-access memory—RAM**, and auxiliary (or secondary) memory, known as **read-only memory—ROM**. Main memory holds the instructions and data used when a program is running. Auxiliary memory holds data and programs not in use.

The first commercial computer

The Williams-Kilburn tube worked well and, by 1949, Baby had been scaled up into a more powerful and reliable computer: the Manchester Mark 1. A magnetic drum was added, which could store data on a series of magnetic tracks that were "read" when the information was needed. It was the forerunner of the modern computer's hard drive. From this, the first commercially produced computer, the Ferranti Mark 1, was developed. Nine of these were built and sold.

Whirlwind

The Whirlwind computer, developed at MIT (the Massachusetts Institute of Technology), went into operation in 1951. It was the first computer to use a new kind of memory, developed by Professor Jay Forrester. It stored memory on tiny magnets fixed on a wire grid. This was known as magnetic core memory, and it soon replaced punched cards and vacuum tubes.

Whirlwind was the first computer to respond almost instantly to instructions, and to show its results on a video screen. By now, computers were so much improved that it was clear that they could have a range of uses other than just mathematical calculations.

The Whirlwind on display at the Museum of Science in Boston, Massachusetts. Its magnetic core memory allowed it to run twice as fast as earlier computers—although it was still extremely slow by modern standards.

Breakthrough

Fast-running computers could now store their own programs, and operating in real time had become a reality.

The transistor

The second age of the computer

By the late 1940s and early 1950s, computer science had come a long way, but it was still dependent on clumsy and unreliable vacuum tubes as a way of controlling the flow of electrical currents through computers. The tube was by then 40 years old: for the next step, something smaller and much faster was needed.

Invention of the transistor

John Bardeen, William Shockley, and Walter Brattain were scientists at the Bell Telephone Laboratories in New Jersey. There, vacuum tubes were used to boost, or amplify, the signals that carried long-distance telephone calls. Shockley and Brattain had been working on more efficient amplifier designs since the 1930s. They were using **semiconductors**, but without any success until Bardeen, a theoretical physicist, found out where they had been going wrong. Bardeen and Brattain worked together and, on December 16, 1947, they succeeded in inventing the "point-contact transistor" (a small, reliable device for controlling

Semiconductors

Certain materials, such as metals, are conductors, which means electricity can pass easily through them. Others, such as plastics, are insulators, which electricity cannot pass through. Semiconductors have properties somewhere between the insulators and conductors. Adding certain substances to a semiconductor makes it possible to control how electricity passes through it.

William Shockley

Date of birth: February 13, 1910

Place of birth: London, England

Profession: Physicist

Greatest achievement: The invention of the transistor, with John Bardeen and Walter Brattain

Interesting fact: As well as a brilliant physicist, Shockley was also an amateur magician. He once magically produced a bunch of roses during a talk for the American Physical Society.

Date of death: August 12, 1989

This is the world's first transistor, made in 1947. It consisted of a plastic triangle suspended above a crystal of the semiconducting material, germanium. A strip of gold was wrapped around the triangle, and this carried the electric current, which the semiconductor can amplify (make stronger).

electric current). It was used in the first successful semiconductor amplifier. The three researchers were awarded the 1956 Nobel Prize in Physics for the invention of the transistor.

THAT'S A FACT!

In May 1948 Bell Laboratories' electrical engineer and science fiction writer John Robinson Pierce came up with the name "transistor"—a combination of "transfer" and "resistor," for the new devices.

Small and reliable

Thanks to Bardeen, Shockley, and Brittain, the lightbulb-sized vacuum tube was replaced by a device smaller than a fingernail. The invention of the small, reliable transistors brought in the Second Age of Computing. They were first used in hearing aids and portable radios, but it wasn't long before computer companies recognized their potential. In the 1950s, IBM and other companies started using transistors in their computers. Because they used little power and were small, transistors could be packed into a small space without any worries about overheating—something impossible with vacuum tubes.

"The combined results of several people working together is often much more effective than could be that of an individual scientist working alone."
John Bardeen, 1972

Breakthrough

Transistors opened the way for computers to become smaller, more powerful, more portable, and, as a result, more widespread. A computer in every business was, at last, about to become a reality.

UNIVAC

The first business computers

Computers had become reliable and smaller, and could now perform a range of tasks—including record-keeping as well as their traditional role of calculating. It was not long before businesses began to demand them.

Census again

In 1946, the United States Census Bureau commissioned Mauchly and Eckert, who had built ENIAC (see page 22), to design and build a new computer. This was the Universal Automatic Computer (UNIVAC), which became one of the first computers used chiefly by business. Progress was slow: the design wasn't finished until 1948 and the Bureau didn't take delivery of it until March 1951.

UNIVAC was different from ENIAC in several ways. It was built as a stored program computer and it used a keyboard and magnetic tape (plastic tape coated with magnetic metal) for inputting data.

John Presper Eckert

John Presper Eckert (right) with the codesigner of UNIVAC, John W. Mauchly.

Date of birth: April 9, 1919

Place of birth: Philadelphia, Pennsylvania

Profession: Electrical engineer

Greatest achievement: Co-inventor of the UNIVAC and ENIAC computers

Interesting fact: Eckert's father was a millionaire, but he claimed that he couldn't afford to send his son to study at MIT. When Eckert discovered his father's deceit he became depressed and almost failed his first year of study at Moore Engineering School.

Date of death: June 3, 1995

THAT'S A FACT!

In a 1952 publicity stunt, the UNIVAC computer was used to predict the results of the race for the presidency between Dwight Eisenhower and Adlai Stevenson. UNIVAC predicted a landslide victory for Eisenhower, but other polls disagreed and the news media declared that the computer's predictive powers were a flop. In fact, UNIVAC proved to be right to within 1 percent of the actual result. Once people discovered this, UNIVAC quickly became a household name.

General Dwight D. Eisenhower, nicknamed Ike, campaigning in the 1952 election. Data collected before the election and used by the new UNIVAC computer accurately predicted an Eisenhower victory—despite widespread expectations that he would lose.

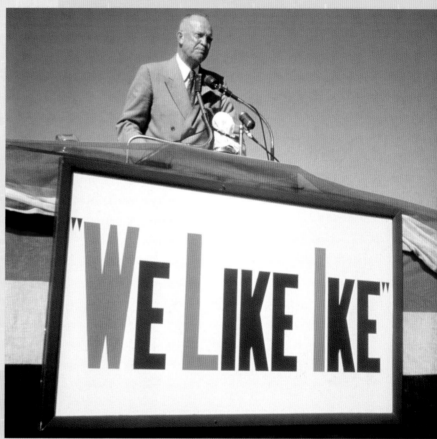

This was much faster than the punched cards still being used by IBM's computers. But it was still huge: it weighed around 14 tons (13 t) and took up more than 375 square feet (35 sq m) of floor space.

The beginning of mass-produced computers

UNIVAC had been designed as a data processing machine for business. Forty-six UNIVAC computers were built, priced at up to $1.5 million each. They were used by both government and commercial organizations, including the United States Navy and Air Force, US Steel, and many insurance companies.

Breakthrough

Because of UNIVAC's success in predicting the 1952 election result, huge numbers of people became aware of computers and what they could do.

The microchip arrives

The limits of transistors

Transistors increased the complexity of the circuits that could be fitted into a computer. But, although transistors were small, they still had to be big enough to be wired by hand.

The tyranny of numbers

Putting all the components together was a tricky, time-consuming task, especially as the components had to be as small as possible and the wires connecting them had to be short (so that the electric signals could travel between them quickly). There were so many components and circuits in an advanced computer that it became next to impossible to build. This problem was known as the "tyranny of numbers."

Jack Kilby and Robert Noyce

In 1958, Jack Kilby, an engineer at Texas Instruments, had the idea of making all the components of a circuit out of a single

This very first integrated circuit was made in 1958, and consisted of a transistor and a few other components on a wafer-thin piece of germanium, a semiconductor. It was barely more than half an inch long, but it revolutionized the electronics industry.

Jack Kilby

Date of birth: November 8, 1923

Place of birth: Jefferson City, Missouri

Profession: Electronics engineer

Greatest achievement: The invention of the integrated circuit

Interesting fact: Jack Kilby designed the first pocket calculator, called the Pocketronic.

Date of death: June 20, 2005

The Third Age

With microchips, there was no more need for tricky hand-assembly. Circuits could be made smaller and their manufacture could be automated. This was the beginning of the "third age" of computers. Computing power that once needed a roomful of vacuum tubes could now be held in the palm of the hand.

"What we didn't realize then was that the integrated circuit would reduce the cost of electronic functions by a factor of a million to one, nothing had ever done that for anything before."
Jack Kilby, 1997

Jack Kilby received the 2000 Nobel Prize in Physics for the invention of the microchip. Robert Noyce went on to cofound Intel, one of the world's largest producers of microchips.

block of semiconducting material with metal connections drawn by machine and added as a layer on top. This was the first **integrated circuit**, or **microchip**.

In January 1959, Robert Noyce, cofounder of the Fairchild Semiconductor Corporation, came up with an idea that was similar to Kilby's. He wrote a detailed application for a patent and was awarded one while Kilby's earlier application was still being considered.

THAT'S A FACT!

The Stardust space probe, launched in 1999 to the comet Wild 2 and back, carried the names of more than a million people electronically engraved on a microchip. The writing is so small that about 80 letters equals the width of a human hair.

GUI and the mouse

Information space

Years before the **Internet** and the World Wide Web existed, Douglas Engelbart imagined a time when people's computer displays would be the window into an "information space." He went on to completely change the way people worked with computers.

NLS

Engelbart was truly ahead of his time. In 1963, he set up his own research laboratory, called the Augmentation Research Center, at the Stanford Research Institute in California. Throughout the 1960s and 1970s his laboratory developed a system called NLS (oNLine System). NLS marked a number of significant breakthroughs in computing, by suddenly making it all much easier.

NLS pioneered the first successful use of **hypertext**. Hypertext is what allows you to

click through from one page to another on the Internet. The function is often highlighted on the screen in some way.

NLS created new **graphical user interfaces** (GUIs) that allowed users to communicate with the computer through icons on the screen rather than by typing in instructions. It could run more than one application

Pages on the Internet can be linked with each other using highlighted "hypertext" words. The computer user knows that clicking on a highlighted word, or link, will open a new page of information.

Hypertext

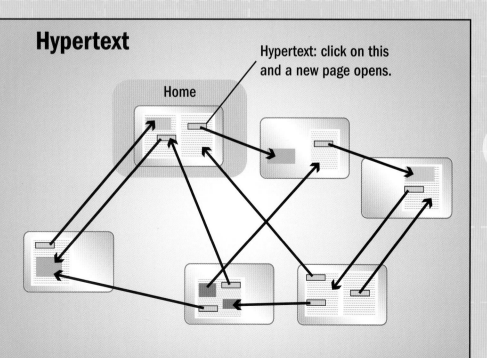

Hypertext: click on this and a new page opens.

Home

Douglas Engelbart

Date of birth: January 30, 1925

Place of birth: Portland, Oregon

Profession: Inventor and computer engineer

Greatest achievement: Developing the NLS computer system

Interesting fact: In 1988, Engelbart founded the Doug Engelbart Institute with his daughter Christina. It aims to find better ways for people to work together to solve important problems.

The mouse

NLS also made use of a new device Engelbart had invented—the mouse. Engelbart's original mouse (in his hand above) was a wooden shell with two metal wheels. It was called a "mouse" because, as Engelbart said, "the tail came out the end." The mouse came into general use in the 1980s, when Apple computers began using them.

Englebert's mouse, designed in the late 1960s, had a wooden shell. Today, a mouse made from plastic is a feature on most personal computers, and is designed to slide over surfaces rather than run on wheels.

at the same time, each one in a different "window" on the screen. NLS provided several word processing options (ways of using a computer as a typewriter) and even provided for on-screen video teleconferencing.

All of these innovations, which today we take entirely for granted, amazed computer users of the time.

Breakthrough

The mouse and on-screen graphics made computers much more "user-friendly"—paving the way for home computing to become popular.

Internet dawn

An idea for a network

In the 1960s, scientists began to work on the idea of using computers over a network, so that computer power could be shared by many users. This was the beginning of what we now call the Internet.

ARPAnet

The first computer network was ARPAnet (Advanced Research Projects Agency), part of the US Defense Department. Its goal was to allow researchers access to large, powerful computers, even if they were far away. There were early links between the University of California, Los Angeles (UCLA), and Doug Engelbart's laboratory at the Stanford Research Institute. By September 1973, 40 computer laboratories were on the network, which began to expand globally.

The network spreads

As ARPAnet grew, tools such as e-mail and file transfers from one computer to another soon followed. The first e-mail was sent in late 1971 by Ray Tomlinson of the technology company Bolt, Beranek, and Newman.

NSFnet

In 1986, the National Science Foundation Network (NSFnet) was set up. Eventually, every major college in the United States was linked to NSFnet, which formed the basis of today's Internet. By 1990, it had taken over from the slower ARPAnet, which was shut down. Commercial companies linked up in 1988 and, with the advent of the personal computer, ordinary people started getting involved, too.

Ray Tomlinson

Date of birth: April 23, 1941
Place of birth: Amsterdam, New York
Profession: Computer programmer
Greatest achievement: The invention of e-mail, in 1971.
Interesting fact: The first e-mail sent announced that e-mail existed—but it was not saved and no one can remember the exact words used.

TCP/IP

"Transmission Control Protocol/Internet Protocol" (TCP/IP) was designed in 1982, as a way of sending data from one computer to another on the network:

- The transmitting computer uses IP to break its data into a number of digital "packets."
- TCP makes sure the packets are delivered in the right order.

Today, we use the Internet to tap into information held on computers all over the world. In just 20 years the Internet has grown from a tool for scientists to an indispensable part of our lives.

THAT'S A FACT!

The first "spam e-mail" was sent on May 3, 1978, advertising a new DEC computer. There are now several billion such messages sent every day.

Breakthrough

ARPAnet proved that computers could be linked together over long distances and led directly to the Internet, invented less than 10 years later.

The microprocessor

Integrated circuits

The invention of integrated circuits completely changed computer design. However, researchers still continued to look for ways to make computers even smaller and more powerful.

Intel 4004

In 1968, two engineers, Robert Noyce (co-inventor of the microchip) and Gordon Moore set up a new company called Intel (short for Integrated Electronics). A year later, a Japanese company called Busicom asked Intel to design 12 microchips to be used for different functions in a calculator that Busicom were manufacturing.

Intel engineer Ted Hoff suggested that, instead of building 12 chips, they built one chip that could do the job of 12. Together with designers Federico Faggin and Stan Mazor, who wrote the software, Hoff set to work. Nine months later they had the world's first single chip **microprocessor**—the Intel 4004.

The microprocessor changed computing beyond recognition. Today, microprocessors are tiny and are used in everyday appliances, from televisions to microwaves.

Robert Noyce

Date of birth: December 12, 1927

Place of birth: Burlington, Iowa

Profession: Electronics engineer

Greatest achievement: Co-inventor of the integrated circuit.

Interesting fact: Noyce was very nearly expelled from college when he stole a pig from a local farmer for a college feast.

Date of death: June 3, 1990

THAT'S A FACT!

The 4004 chip was just 0.12 inches (0.3 cm) wide and 0.16 inches (0.4 cm) long—but it was as powerful as ENIAC.

The invention of the microprocessor allowed thousands of tiny transistors and other electrical components to be packed into chips around one tenth of an inch across, which were made of silicon, a semiconducting material.

Computer brain

The microprocessor, which contains the computer's computation and control systems, is often called a **central processing unit (CPU)**. It is the computer's "brain." All that need to be added are a power supply, memory, and **peripherals**—such as a keyboard and mouse—that allow the user to send commands to the CPU.

The microprocessor may well be the single most complex object ever to be mass-produced. By 2009, CPUs were being produced that had 800 million transistors (compared with the Intel 4004's 2,300). Some researchers believe that by 2015, 15 billion transistors could be packed into a single CPU.

Breakthrough

The invention of the microprocessor paved the way for smaller and smaller, but increasingly powerful, computers to be built. Without microprocessors, laptops and palmtop computing would be impossible.

Computing gets personal

Today, computers are everywhere. They have become such an important part of everyday life that it is hard to imagine that, only 40 years ago, computers were not found in people's homes at all.

The Altair

By the late 1970s, there was a growing demand for computers people could use at home. Oddly, the big computer companies failed to notice this at first. Then, in 1975, a company called MITS started selling computers in kit form for home assembly. The company's Altair was the first successful do-it-yourself personal computer. It used Intel's new 8080 microprocessor. Assembling the computer and writing software for it were left to the buyer. As it was intended for enthusiasts, its makers were amazed when thousands were sold in the first few months.

BASIC and Microsoft

A student called Bill Gates bought an Altair. Together with programmer Paul Allen, he put together a version of BASIC, a type of computer language, that would run on the Altair. Allen became Director of Software at MITS and Gates worked there part-time. In November 1975, Gates and Allen formed a partnership called Micro-Soft, which later became simply Microsoft. By 2008, Microsoft dominated the world software market and had a global annual revenue of more than $60 billion.

The IBM PC

Five years after the Altair was first launched, IBM at last realized that there was a market for computers in the home. The firm launched the IBM PC (personal computer) and asked Bill Gates to write the operating system for it. IBM sold 500,000 PCs in just two years.

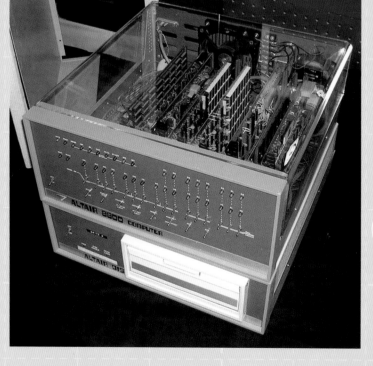

An Altair computer from the 1970s. This model, used for display purposes, has had part of its casing replaced with transparent material. Computers like this were sold mainly to enthusiasts, who assembled them and wrote their own software.

Bill Gates

Date of birth: October 28, 1955

Place of birth: Seattle, Washington

Profession: Chairman of Microsoft

Greatest achievement: Founded Microsoft, one of the biggest companies in the world.

Interesting fact: Bill Gates, one of the world's richest men, has given nearly $30 billion to charity.

THAT'S A FACT!

The first IBM PC came with just 16Kb of memory. Today, many computers have at least 250,000 times that!

A Technological Revolution

At work and at home, personal computers brought about a Technological Revolution that was every bit as important as the Industrial Revolution of 200 years earlier. Before personal computers were introduced into offices, letters had to be typed on manual or electronic typewriters. These allowed for minor corrections to be made, but any big mistakes meant the whole document had to be torn up and typed again.

The computer also revolutionized banking, printing, design, accounting, and many other businesses. Complex arithmetic could be carried out and accurate figures produced at the touch of a button. Industrial processes could be managed by computers using robots to carry out the repetitive tasks previously done by people.

At home, computers enabled people to type and print their own letters, store home accounts, and, soon, play increasingly complicated video games. Meanwhile, computers were finding their way into many pieces of essential home equipment, from cars to washing machines.

Breakthrough

With the IBM PC, personal computing became a reality, and it wasn't long before everyone wanted one. The personal computer changed home and working life for ever.

A world connected

Computers everywhere

The invention of the World Wide Web accelerated the use of computers both in homes and in businesses. In 2009, it was estimated that a quarter of the world's 6.7 billion people had access to the Internet. This has freed businesses from having to rely on mail and shipping services to share documents. Instead of possibly waiting days for a delivery, a file can now be sent across the world in moments.

Hypertext and the World Wide Web

Douglas Englebart had successfully demonstrated hypertext links way back in 1968. **Hypermedia** (linking text, sounds, and visuals) followed. The first hypermedia application was the Aspen Movie Map in 1977, which allowed the user to take a virtual tour of the town of Aspen, Colorado. In 1980, Tim Berners-Lee at CERN, the European Organization for Nuclear Research, created ENQUIRE, a hypertext database for use by fellow researchers.

Sir Timothy Berners-Lee

Date of birth: June 8, 1955

Place of birth: London, England

Profession: Computer scientist

Greatest achievement: The invention of the World Wide Web.

Interesting fact: In June 2007, Sir Timothy Berners-Lee was awarded the Order of Merit by Queen Elizabeth II. Only 24 living people are allowed to hold this honor at any time.

At the end of the 1980s Berners-Lee saw a way to link hypertext with the Internet, so that scientists around the world could share their research. This grew to become the World Wide Web.

One world—one web

Computers and the Internet have transformed our lives. Today, billions of people share their ideas, work, buy goods

Today computers perform an incredible variety of functions in our daily lives, from simply helping us to keep in contact with friends, to vitally important tasks such as ensuring the safety of aircraft.

The power and portability of modern computers would have amazed the pioneers of 60 years ago. Wireless connection allows us to access the vast source of information on the Internet, and to communicate with other computers from almost anywhere.

and services, and organize their social lives via the web. Search engines such as Google, Yahoo, and Bing have become vital tools for navigating the staggering amounts of information that are available on the Internet. With a few clicks of a mouse it is possible to get a weather forecast, have instant access to world news, download music, share photographs and videos, catch up on television shows, and talk face-to-face with relations abroad.

Full speed to the future

The speed with which computers process information is limited by the time it takes for the electrical signals to pass from one electronic component to another.

Scientists are now developing ways of sending the signals between components in the form of light. These optical computers will have greater speed and processing power than ever. The fastest computer in the world today is the IBM Roadrunner at the Los Alamos National Laboratory, New Mexico. It can perform a thousand trillion operations every second. With optical technology, some

researchers believe, future computers could run a billion times faster.

All of this computing power will open up possibilities, such as computers that react to hand and eye movements, that just a few years ago might have seemed fantastic. Intelligent computers that find their own ways to solve problems may soon become a reality.

THAT'S A FACT!

An hour of calculations on an optical computer would be the equivalent of 11 years on an electronic model.

Breakthrough

The invention of the World Wide Web allowed access to the Internet for all. This has revolutionized the way that we live and work.

Glossary

abacus a type of counting frame with beads that slide on wires

artificial intelligence the part of computer science that deals with making machines that can mimic human thought processes

binary number system a number system used by computers in which every number can be represented using only 0 and 1

cathode ray tube a vacuum tube in which a beam of electrons is focused on to a phosphorescent screen, causing it to glow. Early televisions used cathode ray tubes to form the images displayed.

central processing unit (CPU) the part of a computer that carries out its programs

code a way of sending a message so that only the people it is intended for can understand it

computation the process by which a number is found as the result of figuring out a sum

computer programming developing a sequence of instructions to be carried out by a computer

electric charge a quantity of electricity that flows in electric currents or that accumulates on surfaces

graphical user interface a type of computer display that allows the user to operate the computer by moving and clicking icons on the screen

hypermedia a multimedia system in which graphics, text, and sound can all be linked together

hypertext text displayed on a computer screen that links to other text, usually reached by a mouse click

incandescent lightbulb a lightbulb that worked by running electricity through a very fine thread called a filament, which created heat and bright light

Industrial Revolution the period of history in the late 18th and early 19th centuries when developments in technology led to a rise in mechanization and the production of goods in factories

integrated circuit a miniature electronic circuit made from a single piece of semiconducting material

Internet the worldwide network of computers

logarithms a system of tables (lists of numbers) that makes it possible to figure out complicated multiplication sums using addition

memory the part of a computer that stores its data and programs

microchip an integrated circuit

microprocessor a single microchip that holds a computer's whole central processing unit

peripherals devices, such as printers, that are connected to a computer

probability the likelihood that an event will take place; the probability of getting heads on a coin toss is one in two

programmer someone who writes programs for computers

punched card a card on which data is recorded in the form of punched holes

random-access memory the part of a computer's memory used to perform tasks by active programs

read-only memory the part of a computer that stores programs and data in a permanent form

relay an electrical switch that is opened and closed by an electrical circuit

semiconductor a substance that has electrical properties between those of a conductor and an insulator

software computer programs

transistor a semiconductor device used in electrical circuits to switch or amplify current

vacuum tube an electronic device, also called a valve, used to create, switch, or amplify an electrical signal, or current

Further information

Books

Ada Lovelace: The Computer Wizard of Victorian England by Lucy Lethbridge. Short Books Ltd, 2004.

Artificial Intelligence by Harry Henderson. Chelsea House, 2007.

Computers by Anne Rooney. Heinemann-Raintree, 2006.

How Computers Work by Ron White, and Timothy Edward Downs. QUE, 2007.

Jacquard's Web by James Essinger. OUP, 2007.

Tim Berners-Lee by Stephanie Sammartino McPherson. 21st Century Books, 2009.

Some useful web sites

The Analytical Engine
www.fourmilab.ch/babbage/contents.html
Lots of information about the Analytical Engine.

The Case Files: Herman Hollerith
www.fi.edu/learn/case-files/hollerith
Find out about Herman Hollerith and his invention.

Take a tour of Bletchley Park
www.lightstraw.co.uk/bletchley/tour.html
Information about Bletchley Park and the Colossus Rebuild Project.

ENIAC Museum Online
www.seas.upenn.edu/~museum
Find out how ENIAC was built.

MouseSite
sloan.stanford.edu/MouseSite/1968Demo.html#complete
Watch Douglas Engelbart's legendary demonstration of NLS.

A brief history of the Internet
www.walthowe.com/navnet/history.html
Information about the development of the Internet and e-mail.

Index